Book Title:

IOl41778

Shoeing the Whole Horse-Not just the hoof: A guide for the horse owner.

THANK YOU FOR YOUR PURCHASE... We hope you enjoy this book.
If this book contains any print errors, contact customer service for a free replacement copy.
We are dedicated to providing you a quality product for an affordable price.

Published by:

FARRIER-FRIENDLY™ **SERVICES**

Athens, OH 45701

Website: www.farrierfriendly.com
Email: farrierfriendly@hotmail.com

. _____ *A Special Thanks to* : _____ .

The family of King Lamadora, Dr. Doug Butler and Kirk Underschultz for their permission to reprint some of their illustrations—and most importantly their friendship and encouragement over the years.

Table of Contents:

Preface :

In every craft there's always a learning curve. When a young farrier begins his or her career they are expected, in short order, to get a grasp of the basics. There will be many highs and lows as a student works to become competent in his/her skills. During the first few years of training, not much time is spent on anything "unusual". Sticking to the basics is a critical part of the learning process and expecting anyone to think "outside-the-box" before they are able to comprehend it, will only lead to confusion and frustration.

As a horse owner, you may have noticed that usually the most experienced of veterinarians or farriers are those that come up with some of the most creative solutions to the most perplexing problems.

For me, it was a decade of practicing the basics of my shoeing craft before I had the great fortune of meeting one of those truly talented farriers. His name, King Lamadora, and he was, in my mind, someone who knew the basics of horseshoeing, but was able to go beyond that to reach "outside-the- box" in order to help solve many of those mysterious lamenesses. Though Mr. Lamadora is no longer with us, many of the concepts in this guide are thoughts that he would often emphasize.

In fact, before his untimely death in 2010, King asked that I never forget and continue to pass the word…
to promote the shoeing of our horses in a manner that will always consider the effect that trimming and shoeing will have on the *whole* horse.

And so, with that came the inspiration to put this guide together. It is with fond memories of my time spent with such a "creativity thinker" as King Lamadora that I continue my journey of learning and it is with this *"Farrier-Friendly"*™ guide that I hope to enlighten you to some new ideas—perhaps, shedding a little light on some of those potential hoof-related lameness issues that may come your way.

Thank you for your interest in *"Farrier-Friendly"*™ and good luck as you continue your journey of learning with your horse.

Your friend in horses,

Bryan Farcus MA,CJF-BWFA

For century's horsemen have recognized the importance of maintaining their horses' feet. Writings by Xenophon the Greek, dating back to *circa* 400 B.C. discuss the importance of a healthy frog and a hard hoof wall. The first evidence of attempting to shoe horses is uncertain, despite evidence of blacksmithing recorded in the bible under Genesis 4:22. As the craft of horseshoeing evolved there were those who misinterpreted it as a form of witchcraft and many horsemen would express contempt and cynicism for the chaotic situations that resulted. As we move into a new millennium, in many respects the horsemen of today often experience a somewhat similar, yet far less dramatic, form of doubt. Unfortunately, despite advancements in our diagnostic abilities, we may have digressed in our

capability to read a horse as a *whole*. From the first
Cavalry manual on horseshoeing to the more traditional farrier science textbooks, the understanding of how to evaluate the entire horse for shoeing has eluded us. Of course, there has always been a general reference to conformation but how to view the top line of a horse and draw relations to the baseline or hooves has not been scrutinized enough. However, on a more positive note, with an ever-increasing demand for our horses to live longer, more prosperous lives, the idea of shoeing for a "Proper Balance Movement™" is gaining the interest of many modern day horse owners and with this trend I believe that the quality of our horse care can only get better.

Have you ever heard the saying, "sometimes you can't see the forest due to the trees"? As horse owners, perhaps, we suffer from this affliction. It has been my experience that we can overlook some details when it comes to our horses. When it comes to the shoeing of your horse, you should be aware of two important details. The first is his way of standing and the other is his way of going. Becoming aware of a more properly balanced stance and movement, helps us get to know our horses in a more intimate manner. Quite often horses do not move in the same manner in which they stand. For instance, it is common to notice that horses with a base-narrow stance will move wider. Conversely, those with base-wide stances often move narrow. In many instances, too many farriers will routinely walk-up to a horse, pick-up his feet and shoe each foot and leave. Unfortunately,

they could be missing a wealth of information.

Watching how horses posture as they travel, how their

feet land (concussion force) and also how the hooves

bear weight (compression force) will help a farrier

achieve the best "horse-balance" possible.

Traditionally, hoof balance has been viewed with a

classical reference. Hoof-to- pastern angles, matching

toe lengths, hairline assessments, T-square views and

hoof wall symmetry are helpful but they only show

one side of the Proper BalanceMovement™ equation.

These references alone can be limiting. Looking

above and beyond, towards your horse's top line will

open a field of view that will allow you to see the

whole horse from a new prospective. Examining the

levelness of your horse's shoulders, knees, hips, hocks

and fetlocks will

awaken you to any disparities. Practicing this kind of

awareness can be helpful when attempting to solve a

puzzling lameness.

As a mentor, as well as a friend, King Lamadora practiced and perfected the concepts of Proper Balance Movement™ for nearly 30 years. During this time, Mr. Lamadora discovered that the approach he found most effective when communicating with horse owners was to initiate the conversation by observing the horse's top-line first and then drawing references to his feet. It seems as though the connection between the horse's feet and his body is understood by the horse owner more easily when approached in this manner.

King's approach offers the following suggestions so that you can build a better awareness of your horse:

➤1. Remember your basics of horseshoeing. Grasping the idea of geometric and dynamic balance is the key to understanding the basic function of your horse's hooves.

➢2. Gain more knowledge of your horse's overall conformation, as it pertains to his anatomy and physiology. This approach to conformation analysis should be from a scientific perspective, rather than a show ring standard.

➢3. From a "bird's eye" view, top-down approach, you should see an even body mass on both sides (symmetrically shaped muscling on right and left sides). Often, you may notice a difference in how he carries his barrel. An appearance of lopsidedness is a common indicator of a weaker conformation, which can translate into what is considered to be a *disconnection* of the horse's feet from his body. Another way to conceptualize this may be by simply realizing that *unbalanced hooves always result in unbalanced bodies and vice versa.* 12

➢4. When horses move well or *sound*, you will see a uniform roll, rise, and return/fall of both the shoulders and the hips. From a profile, you will also notice an even/equal swing of front and hind limbs as your horse tracks forward in his working gait.

➢5. *"Sound horses, sound sound"*... Believe it or not, a good ear can hear whether or not your horse is traveling sound. The cadence of a hoof beat should be very distinct and even, when traveling on a hard surface. (i.e. four clear beats for walk, two clear beats for trot, three beats for canter).

To gain a full appreciation of the importance of all this, Dr. Ted Stashak offers this observation in his book titled, <u>Horseowner's Guide to Lameness</u> :

...the ratio of the top line's components, the curvature of the top line, the strength of loin, the sharpness of withers, the slope to the

croup, and the length of the underline in

relation to the length of back all affect a

horse's movement...A horse with a body that is

a great deal longer than its height often

experiences difficulty in synchronization and

coordination.

Realizing your potential to recognize this

concept of *connectedness* (existence of the above

characteristics and how they are interrelated) is the

first step toward reaching the goal of *connecting* your

horse's feet to his body. What's more, you may even

uncover some solutions to certain lameness concerns.

For centuries, noted equine practitioners have

espoused the theory that a horse's feet are his

foundation; responsible for his overall health. By

and large, this theory remains uncontested. However,

still debated is the *how* of it all. Many believe that [14] it's a mere passive relationship, while others maintain that daily circumstances surrounding our horses play a much more direct or active role. From the earliest assertions by Tony Gonzales to the more recent research/ practices of King Lamadora's PBM II, it has become more evident to us that the relationship between horses' feet and their bodies is more direct, than it is indirect. The essence of PBM is and will always be one that promotes the idea of *working on your horse's feet via his body.*

In our first conversation regarding Proper Balance Movement™(PBM) for your horse, we began by emphasizing an approach that encourages the practice of trimming and/or shoeing with the *whole horse* in mind. Then, we continued with a second discussion that was designed to shed some light on the importance of *connecting* your horse's feet to the rest of his body. Now, in this final installment, we will take a look at how your horse's posture (particularly, from a perspective of crookedness) can influence his balance—*for a good posture is the essence of all good balance.*

Throughout his career, as a successful farrier and equine lameness consultant, King Lamadora developed a unique way of helping horses by the use of his special technique, that includes both farriery and *body work.* King possessed a rare gift, as he

was able to help many people, so that they could help

their horses. To begin, Mr. Lamadora offers us some

insight into identifying a few *sure signs* of

crookedness that may exist within your horse …

Here are some of the most common examples of

crookedness that can be observed on a regular basis:

➢ One shoulder or haunch is visibly "over-muscled"

when compared to its partner.

➢ One shoulder or haunch appears dropped when

compared to its partner; resulting in one being carried

ahead of the other as the horse reaches the extension

phase of a given gait.

➢ The rider experiences the feeling of a "flat-tire",

where one hip or shoulder is "knocked down" or

dropped.

➢ The horse is stiffer to one side as he is circled.

➢ When looking at your *horse* at standstill, it appears that one front hoof is bigger, more flared as the partner hoof is smaller and more upright (clubby). This is most often a classic symptom of LLD (Limb Length Disparity).

➢ When cleaning a hoof from the underside, you notice that the frog is lopsided and extremely compressed to one side.

➢ When looking at the hoof from a rear view, one bulb of a heel is higher than the other; often referred to as *sheared heels*.

➢ You often experience a mild, persistent lameness that can not be precisely explained by a traditional veterinary examination.

   ➢ It seems as tough no amount of adjustment or reconfiguration of padding and saddle can create a lasting fit for your horse.

Developing an eye and gaining an awareness of your horse as a *whole,* from head to toe, is the cornerstone for achieving a well balanced horse. Specifically, it is a means to help you identify any conditions and/or circumstance that your horse may be challenged by, as you strive to obtain your horse's optimal hoof balance. It's, also, important to keep in mind that certain side effects of crookedness in your horse may be a result of physical deformities, which will limit him in certain activities. Some of these limitations, however, may be overcome with the help of a qualified farrier and a follow-up with a methodical rehabilitation program. Perhaps, it all comes down to this simple thought—how well our equine friends can cope in our world, relies upon how much we can learn about his.

Each of us has the ability to become more in tune with our equine partners. Whether you're a professional care provider or horses are your hobby, understanding the importance of connecting your horse's feet to his body can result in your horse remaining sound and healthy for many years to come.

We all have the potential to have healing hands and "connect" with our horses. One of the most important things to remember is to be positive and always approach your horse with the intent to help. Nothing is absolute, but if you learn to strive for attainable goals, you might be surprised how much you can achieve.

Just keep moving forward in balance.

Noticing Limb Length Disparity (*LLD*)...

BELOW: a view of a balanced and symmetrical top-line.

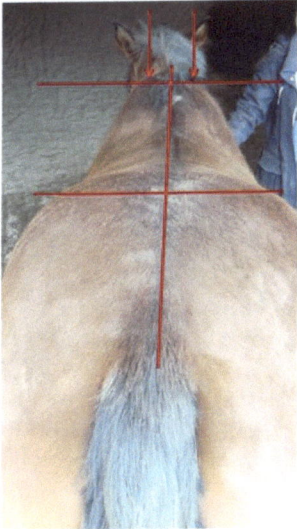

Photo by: Bryan S. Farcus   Learning to view your horse's top-line can offer you a better understanding of why the feet are as they are. Using a top-down approach to assess hoof balance can help a farrier make better trimming and shoeing decisions.

NEXT PAGE (below): a view of a typical dropped shoulder/ but this horse is functionally sound ,as long as he is trimmed and shod to support and promote a more balanced top-line, as opposed to corrective shoeing for the hooves only.

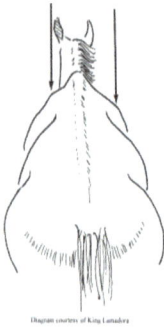

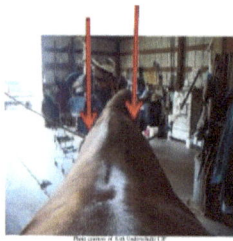

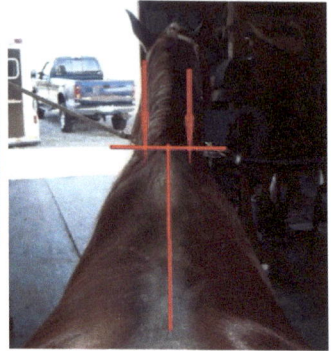

[Above-L]: Before   **[Above-R]: same horse After**

Top-line imbalances can result due to a variety of conformational issues.   Of the most common are: *Club footedness, Low-underrun heels, Curvature of the spine, Dropped shoulder/or hip, Congenital bone length differences within limbs.* Some are functional deviations while others are not.

Scanning on down, you should note any unusual upper limb deviations:

> Most common are **Rotational** (a twisting of a   limb, causing the toe to point inward or out).
> **Angular** (a sharp break in the mechanical alignment of the bones, often appearing off-set in the joints) or **Flexural** (appears that a limb joint is in a fixed state of flex or extension, often appears to be a "benched" or "buckled" joint.

BELOW: a view of a horse representing all three forms of limb deviations.

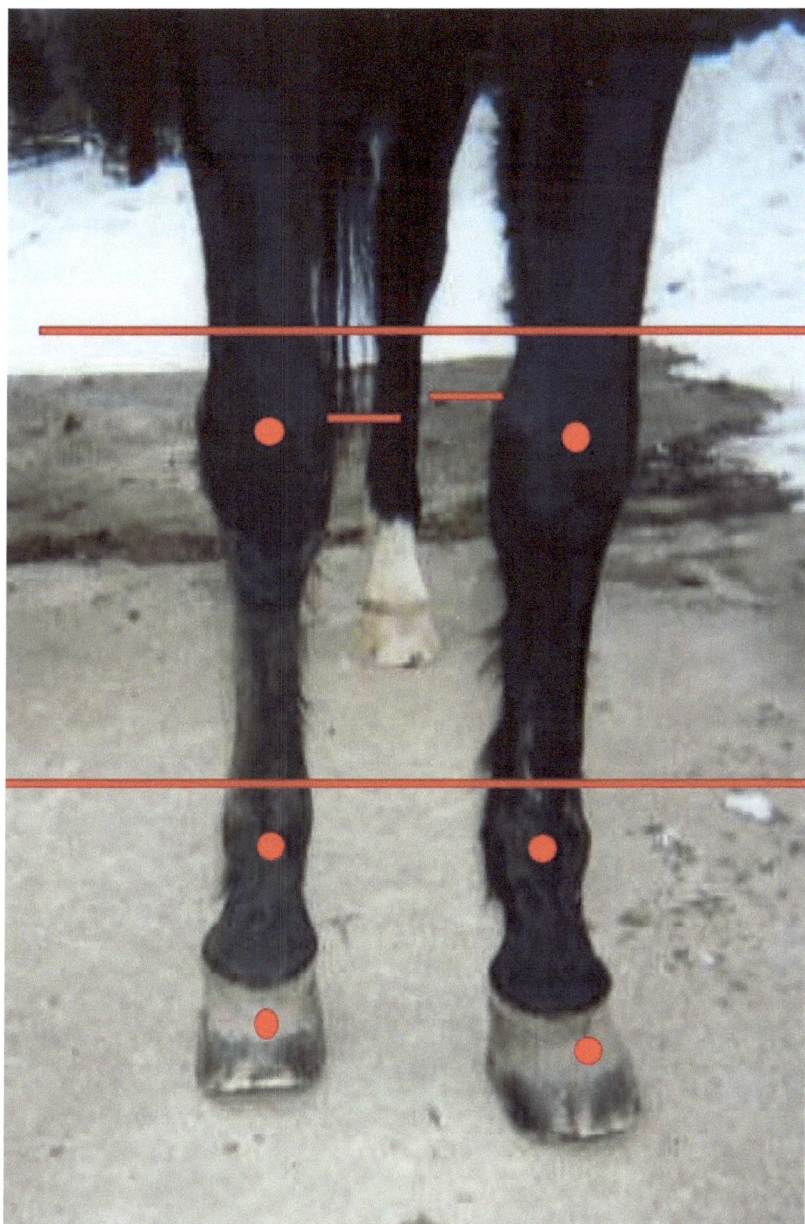

Photo by: Bryan S. Farcus

Glossary of Terms :

Axis BB (Broken-Back): hoof to pastern digit axis line that is visualized to represent a long toe/low heel hoof conformation.

Axis BF (Broken-Forward): hoof to pastern digit axis line that is visualized to represent a short toe/high heel hoof conformation.

Bars: viewed from the bottom of the hoof, minor protrusions present on both sides of the frog, a connective tissue that ties the buttress of the heel to the sole, acts to reinforce the heels.

Bar shoe: general term used to indicate any shoe that is closed or connected at the ends to maximize weight bearing surface, often used to stabilize a weak hoof or support a weakness in a limb.

BBLS: (Basic Body Language System) a term used to identify any system of communicating with the horse through herd instincts, based on predetermined gestures, signals, or cues that are horse logical.

Bulb: located at the back of a hoof connecting the frog and the coronary band, often referred to as the frog band.

Glossary of Terms [continued] :

Buttress of Heel: the part of the hoof wall that runs to the open end of the foot, often referred to as the point or butt of the heel.

Conformation: an overall view of the horse's entire body, comparing the horse's body structure for symmetry and/or functional alignment.

Commissures: the grooves that are present on either side of the frog, sometimes referenced as the paracuneal sulci.

Corrective shoeing: an approach to shoeing with a major emphasis on changing the horse's stance and/or way of going.

Coronary Band: a band of soft tissue that surrounds the top of each hoof nearest the hairline.

Club footed: a hoof that grows excessively high in the heel as compared to the toe length, there are various degrees of severity, generally considered "clubby" if the horse's hoof-to-pastern is broken-forward, due to a flexor tendon contracture that is extreme enough to distend the coffin joint. This condition may be due to an injury, but most commonly inherited.

Glossary of Terms [continued] :

Deep Digital Cushion: also know as the plantar cushion, a fibro-fatty tissue underlying the frog that functions as a shock absorber.

Degree Pad: wedged shaped pads that are placed between the hoof and the shoe that will raise the hoof and lift the rear surface of a limb.

Deviation: a departure from a predetermined ideal, a term often used in horse conformation analysis to describe crookedness in a limb.

Dynamic Hoof Balance: evaluation of hoof balance as it pertains to the horse in motion, considering how the hoof will land and load.

Frog: a triangular shaped, elastic pad-like tissue that is located at the bottom of the foot that acts to absorb concussion and aid in traction

Gait: a pattern of movement or the way in which the horse travels, certain gaits are natural to all horses but some can be artificial.

Hoof Anatomy: the study of the structure/parts of a hoof.

Hoof Physiology: the study of the function of a hoof.

Interfering: a term used to describe the hitting together of a horse's foot to an opposing limb in a manner that restricts the horse's ability to move forward in a comfortable manner.

Keratination: a process whereby the division of horn producing cells accumulate to produce outer layers of hoof wall to protect sensitive tissue, similar to our own nail growth.

LLD (Limb Length Disparity): a condition where the horse suffers from a structural difference of his limbs as a working pair, often a curvature of the spine and/or a clubbed footed conformation is present.

Low-Underrun Heels: When viewed from the side, the heels of the horse are collapsed and low to the ground, the slope or angle of the heel is much lower than that of the toe.

Phalanx -1st : the first bone in the lower limb directly below the fetlock, also known as the long pastern.

Glossary of Terms [continued] :

Phalanx -2nd: the second bone in the lower limb directly below the fetlock, also known as the short pastern.

Phalanx -3rd: the third and last bone in the lower limb directly below the fetlock, also known as the coffin bone.

Quarter: when viewed from the bottom of the hoof, the region of hoof wall that is between the toe and heel.

Sensitive Laminae: an interlocking, velcro-like tissue within a hoof that is responsible for connecting the hoof wall to the coffin bone.

Seat of corn: viewed from the bottom of the hoof, a junction where the edge of the bar, sole and white-line come together, an area susceptible to attracting debris that can result in a sore spot (corn).

Sole: the flat, ground surface portion of the hoof, responsible for creating a natural pad that is designed to protect the coffin bone.

Static Hoof Balance: a view of hoof balance when the

Glossary of Terms [continued] :

---

horse is at a stand still, using a geometric reference (X,Y,Z planes) for a three dimensional perspective.

Supportive Shoeing: fitting a shoe with enough length and width to protect and support the entire limb.

Therapeutic Shoeing: an approach to shoeing that provides a level of comfort and also attempts to remedy a hoof disease.

Vertical Depth Tolerance: a general reference to the amount of exfoliated sole that is able to be safely trimmed without causing the horse to be tender.

White line: usually yellowish or brown, it is the connective tissue (terminal ends of the sensitive laminea) that bonds the hoof wall to the sole, aids in nail placement.

Helpful Tables & Graphics:

This page is reprinted with permission from the
Author of
HORSE FOOT CARE
By Dr. Doug Butler

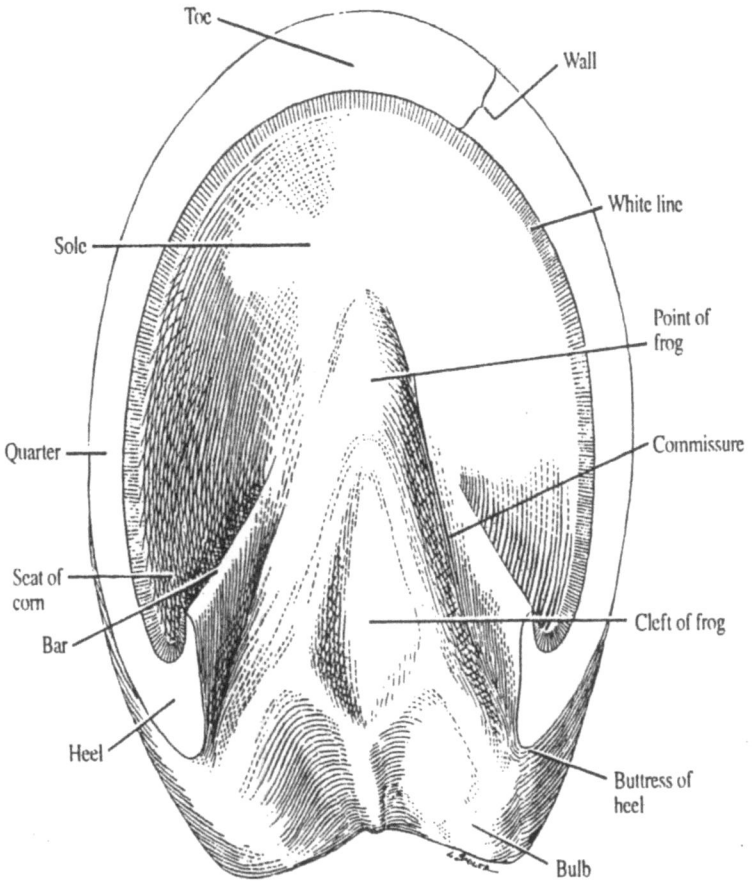

Toe

Wall

White line

Sole

Point of frog

Quarter

Commissure

Seat of corn

Cleft of frog

Bar

Heel

Buttress of heel

Bulb

The parts of the hoof

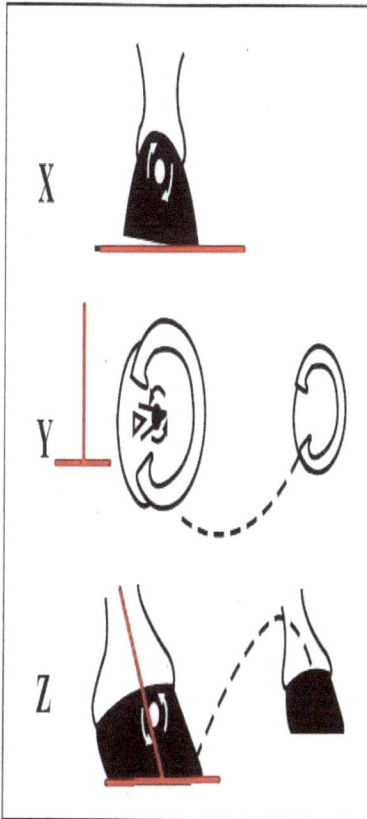

Reprinted by permission: © 1998 Dr. Doug Butler. Shoeing In Your Right Mind

Visualing the 3 dimensions of balance as applied to Dynamic or Functional balance.

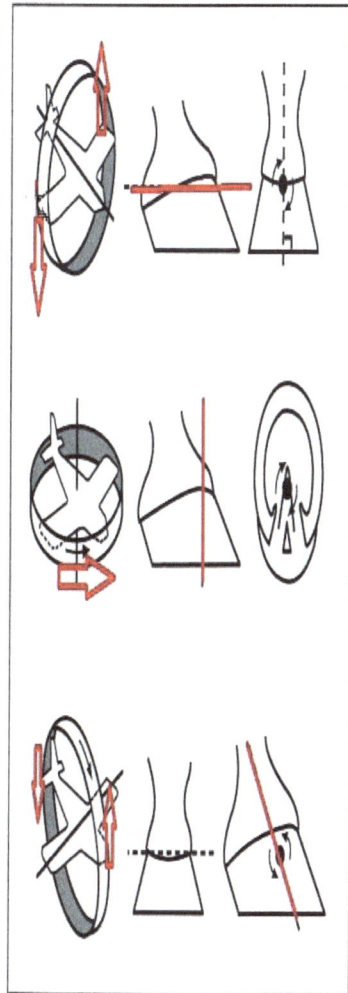

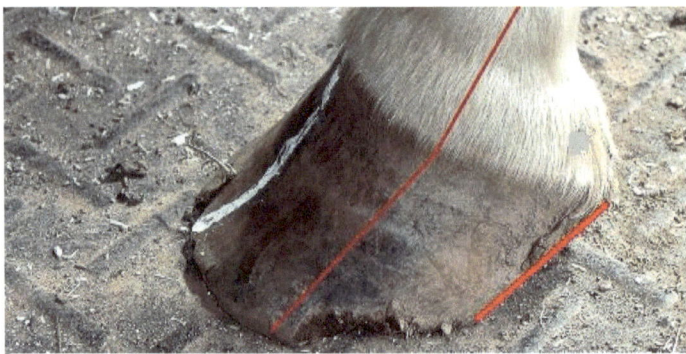

Broken-Back Axis

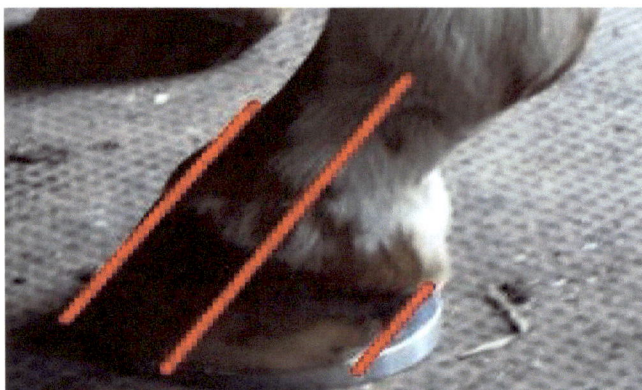

Balanced

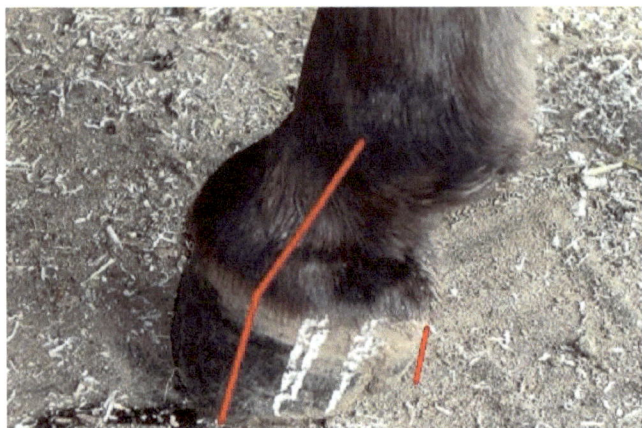

Broken-Forward Axis

Photos by: Bryan Farcus CJF

A POSITIVE *"A Healthy Hoof"*	ITS OPPOSITE *"An Unhealthy Hoof"*
Hard/shiny exterior hoof wall.	Soft/cracked, dull exterior wall.
Symmetrically shaped hoof wall.	Asymmetrically shaped hoof wall.
Soft/flexible hair line tissues.	Hard/"crusty" hair line tissues.
Soft/flexible frog tissues.	Hard or diseased frog tissues.
Parallel growth pattern of toe and heel lengths.	Reversed growth pattern of toe and heel lengths.
Normal cupping of the sole. (bottom surface of hoof is arched allowing for edge of hoof wall to contact ground first)	Extremely flat or "dropped" sole. (bottom surface of hoof is contacting the ground before edge of hoof wall)
Hoof wall thickness approx. 2 x greater than "white line" thickness.	Hoof wall thickness less than the "white line" thickness (white line distortion)
"White line" region and sole surface adjoin without deep cracks present.	Deep cracks existing between the "white line" region and the sole surface.

©2001, Bryan Farcus

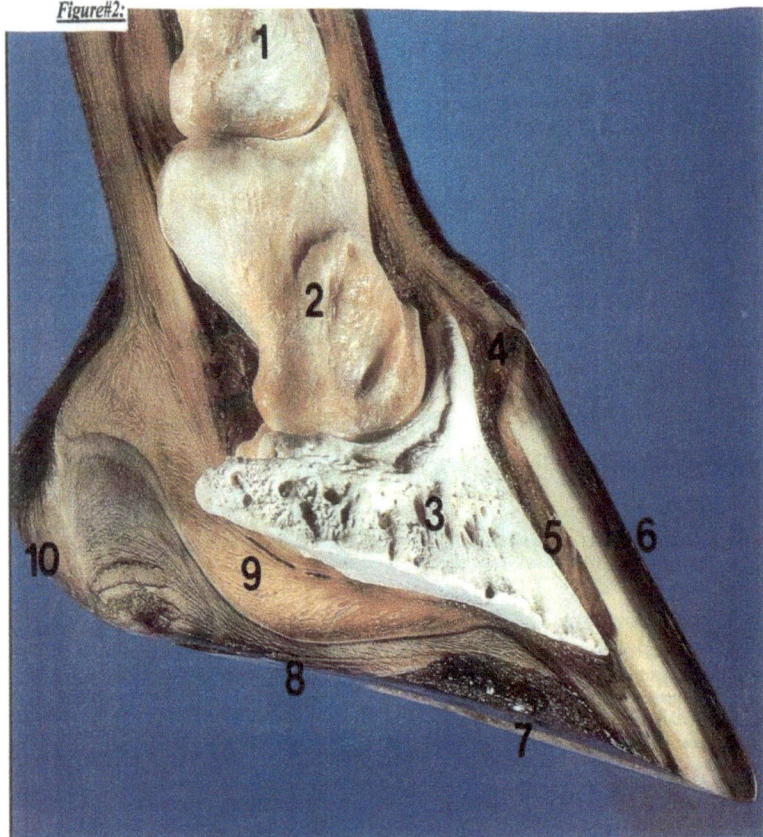

LATERAL OBLIQUE VIEW OF EQUINE DIGIT. Soft tissue is removed from one side of the phalanges.

Used by permission, courtesy of : The American Farriers Journal, ©1999 Lessiter Publications, Inc.

1. First Phalanx (long pastern).
2. Second Phalanx (short pastern).
3. Third Phalanx (coffin bone).
4. Coronary Band.
5. Sensitive Laminae.
6. Hoof wall (toe region).
7. Sole.
8. Frog.
9. Deep Digital Cushion.
10. Bulb of foot.

RESOURCES...

American Farrier's Journal , Lessiter Publications

PBM : A Diary of Lameness, Anthony Gonzales

Shoeing In Your Right Mind , Dr. Doug Butler

Horseowner's Guide to Lameness, Dr. Ted Stashsak

The Principles of Horseshoeing (P3),Doug &Jacob Butler

The Lame Horse , James R. RooneyDVM

WEBSITES...

www.butlerprofessionalfarrierschool.com
www.myhorsematters.com
www.horseshoes.com

ASSOCATIONS...

AAPF, American Association of Professional Farriers, www.professionalfarriers.com

AFA, American Farrier's Association, www.americanfarriers.org

BWFA, Brotherhood of Working Farriers, www.bwfa.net

About The Author :

Bryan S. Farcus *MA, CJF-BWFA* ~

For the past 25 years, Bryan has been combining the skills of horseshoeing, teaching, and riding. He is a Certified Journeyman Farrier through the Brotherhood of Working Farriers Association (BWFA) and also holds a certification in Equine Massage Therapy. Bryan's other accomplishments include both a Master of Arts degree with a specialization in equine education and a Bachelor of Science degree in the area of business.

For more than ten years, Bryan was the director/ instructor of a Farrier Studies program at an international equestrian college and a guest instructor for others, as well.

These days, he continues his teaching by offering various "horsemanship for horseshoeing" programs. Upon invitation, Bryan presents demonstrations and group discussions on basic hoof care and horsemanship, in order to promote the advancement of equine education. Bryan is also the creator of a select line of "*Farrier-Friendly*™" products and currently authors a series of "*Farrier-Friendly*™" articles that appear in horse magazines throughout the US. Bryan currently works with horses and their owners in Ohio and West Virginia. You can visit him at:

www.farrierfriendly.com or e-mail: farrierfriendly@hotmail.com

www.ingramcontent.com/pod-product-compliance
Lightning Source LLC
Chambersburg PA
CBHW041755050426
42443CB00023B/10